How To Research, Write and Publish an Art History Book in American Art

Diane Elizabeth Kelleher

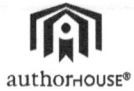

authorHOUSE®

AuthorHouse™
1663 Liberty Drive
Bloomington, IN 47403
www.authorhouse.com
Phone: 1-800-839-8640

First published by AuthorHouse 12/05/2011

ISBN: 978-1-4634-6799-9 (sc)
ISBN: 978-1-4634-6800-2 (ebk)

Library of Congress Control Number: 2011915142

Printed in the United States of America

Any people depicted in stock imagery provided by Thinkstock are models,
and such images are being used for illustrative purposes only.
Certain stock imagery © Thinkstock.

This book is printed on acid-free paper.

Because of the dynamic nature of the Internet, any web addresses or links contained in
this book may have changed since publication and may no longer be valid. The views
expressed in this work are solely those of the author and do not necessarily reflect the
views of the publisher, and the publisher hereby disclaims any responsibility for them.

CONTENTS

INTRODUCTION

Every year, as part of your graduate education in the history of American Art, as a doctoral student, you will be asked to research and write a book. This manual is designed to assist you in this endeavor of eliciting, retrieving, and summarizing data for a topic upon which no pre-existing book is extant.

Had there been such a handbook thirty years ago, when I was researching and writing about the art and life of Lilian Westcott Hale, it would have afforded me a systematic and straightforward ordering of the research methodology process thereby saving me impressive quantities of time and money.

For art historians, knowing how to produce a book from primary and secondary sources is mandatory, not only for graduation from any doctoral program, but for subsequent employment in the field.

Graduate schools in the history of art need to produce art historians, for the public and private sector, capable of writing books from scratch containing biographical, exhibition, and other historical data in a comprehensible straightforward content. This step-by-step manual will save time and money by making the process logical and easy.

This book is divided into three major sections paralleling the tasks inherent in the manual's title:

- research;
- writing; and,
- publishing.

There are certain materials you will need during the course of the research, writing and publishing of your manuscript. These items include:

- one large artist's sketch pad (36" x 24");
- one 1" notebook for correspondance, with tab dividers;
- one 1" notebook for awards and copied critical reviews;
- two 3" notebooks for your text;
- mylar page coverings, one page for each page of text and appendices;
- two to three 1-1/2" notebooks for notes from the Archives of American Art, the Boston Museum School Scrapbooks;
- one notebook and mylar for reproductions (title labels on back) garnered from newspaper articles and your index to reproductions, labelled and separated by tab dividers;
- one 1" notebook for the exhibition history;
- colored paper or three ring notebook tab dividers;
- one 3" notebook to hold transcriptions of interviews, and interview questionnaires;
- one recorder and one transcriber for interviews;
- a computer and a printer for amalgamating the text;
- one camera for taking photographs of patrons' artwork;
- standard office supplies such as pens and pencils, writing paper, computer paper, three hole punch, stapler;
- one box of blank thank you notes.

RESEARCH

THE BEGINNING
The Birth Certificate, the Death Certificate and the Obituary

Research begins at the start of life with the birth certificate and, ironically, at the end of life with the certificate of death. The search begins with your graduate school library's dictionaries of artists and American biography, wherein you are most likely to find a notice of the artist's existance including places and dates of birth and death. The next step is to verify the information obtained by writing to the Bureau of Vital Statistics of the town mentioned for the birth certificate and the death certificate.

After these facts are confirmed, the next step entails a trip to a major public library to ascertain a major newspaper's copy of the artist's obituary. This is usually on microfiche listed by the name of the paper. The newspaper should be chosen on the basis of geographic proximity to the artist's place of birth, death or residence. For Lilian Westcott Hale, for example, this newspaper was *The Boston Herald*. (See Figure 1.) Sometimes, an obituary may also be obtained by writing to the Historical Society of the town mentioned on the death or birth certificate or by writing to the town library which may have its own microfiche or clipping of the local newspaper's notice.

Generally, in addition to dates of birth and death, the obituary offers a wealth of information pertinent to the initial phases of investigation, such as:

- the towns in which the artist recently lived;
- where the artist was buried;
- when the artist was married;
- where the artist was educated;

○ what awards, prizes and medals the artist won;
○ the name of the artist's most well-known
   paintings;
○ where these paintings are currently located;
○ the names of the artist's children and
   grandchildren.

MRS. LILIAN HALE: WAS WIDOW OF NOTED CRITIC

Committal services were held yesterday in Forest Hills Cemetery for Mrs. Lilian Westcott Hale of Charlottesville, Virginia, and Folly Cove, Cape Ann, a noted portrait painter and mother of Nancy Hale, the novelist.

Mrs. Hale died last Thursday at 83 in St. Paul, Minnesota. She was the widow of Philip L. Hale, also a distinguished painter and art critic of The Herald, who died in 1931. Her husband was the son of Edward Everett Hale.

Born in Hartford, Connecticut, she studied there for several years before coming to Boston to work at the Museum of Fine Arts School under the late Edmund Tarbell.

She was married to Mr. Hale in 1902 and for many years resided in Dedham before moving to Charlottesville in 1955.

Her work was nationally recognized, and her portraits of children were a specialty. In 1928, she won the Altman Prize of the National Academy regarded as the highest award in American painting – for her portrait of Taylor Scott Hardin in riding clothes. The Pennsylvania Academy of the Fine Arts awarded her its Beck Medal in 1923.

Last summer, at 83, she won the Annual Rockport Art Association competition.

In addition to Miss Hale, who in private life is Mrs. Fredson Bowers, wife of the Chairman of the English Department of the University of Virginia, she leaves a sister, Mrs. E.G. Littell of St. Paul, two grandsons and three great grandchildren.

Figure 1 –   Obituary of Lilian Westcott Hale taken from the Boston Herald, dated November 13, 1963.

TYING IT ALL TOGETHER
The Chronology

Throughout the course of your research (the surveys, interviews, newspaper articles, correspondances) you will come into the possession of incalculable numbers of facts which need to be organized in a coherent manner.

The best method to accomplish this goal is to first invest in the largest of artists' sketch pads. Then each page can then be divided with a simple ruler and pencil into ten large blocks; the top of each block being labelled with the heading of one specific year. This will yield ten blocks, equivalent to ten years, per large page. Entries are best made noting the month first, then the data. Each page will thus hold the notes for a particular decade. You'll need to make these pages beginning with the year of the artist's birth and continuing at least until the year of his/her death. A miscellaneous spare box can hold notations occurring after death.

Note: *Artists often have posthumous retrospective exhibitions and research publications often appear after an artist has died.*

To make the most of this system, each and every fact or fragment of a fact of the obituary and of all other research which we will explore, needs to be noted under the appropriate year of the chronology. For example, from the obituary we must note that Hale was married in 1902, that she won the Altman Prize in 1928, that her husband died in 1931, and that she moved to Charlottesville, Virginia in 1955.

Note: *All the facts that will appear on the chronology must eventually be verified, for the chronology will form the basis from which you will derive your written text. This means that you will be engaged in large amounts of letter writing, which will necessitate the keeping of correspondence notebooks.*

The Appendices

From the obituary we also begin to derive some of our appendices. These are simply lists of related facts. Here, for example, we see that we need lists for:

- awards, medals and prizes of Lilian Westcott Hale;
- galleries, museums and societies at which she exhibited, including the dates and the titles of her works;
- institutions with which she was associated – educational and otherwise;
- titles of her works;
- relatives and patrons (who may be willing to provide interviews);
- an index to reproductions (in which we note in what library source her art is reproduced); and,
- acknowledgements.

THE CENTRAL FOCUS

The Archives of American Art, The Boston Museum of Fine Arts School Scrapbooks, The Museum of Fine Arts, Boston, Galleries and Institutions, Correspondence and the Interviews

These entities will doubtless constitute the majority of your research focus.

The Archives of American Art

The Archives of American art is located at the top of Beacon Hill, behind the statehouse and the Boston Athenaeum and is accessed by appointment. It houses the papers of innumerable American artists, which have been adapted to rolls of microfilm. These rolls are organized by the name of the institution, for example, as by galleries such as the Guild of Boston Artists, with which a particular artist has exhibited, and also by the artist's last name. Many of these gems of microfilm contain reproductions of actual gallery catalogues of exhibitions which are particularly useful for verifying information gleaned from the Boston Museum of Fine Arts School Scrapbooks. Also included among the memorobilia are genealogical charts, photographs, newspaper articles and, depending on the artist, letters written by and received of the artist.

The Archives is a small facility with only two microfilm machines which is open to scholars Monday through Friday during normal business hours, by appointment. There are no facilities to technologically copy frames from the microfilm, so all data gathering must be done the old fashioned way, by hand. Chances are you will spend many hours at this institution.

Note: *A good way to approach taking notes from this source is to detail, on page one of your day's notes, the frame numbers and title of which section of microfilm you are currently exploring and in addition keep a running master list of frame numbers and subject headings on a separate piece of paper to be used as an index useful later on when you are engaged in the writing and footnoting process.*

Note: *Also keep alphabetized lists of curators and museum and gallery directors mentioned in the text for correspondence and verification purposes in your correspondance notebook.*

The Boston Museum of Fine Arts School Scrapbooks

The Boston Museum of Fine Arts School Scrapbooks are housed at the museum school building on Huntington Avenue, right next to the Museum of Fine Arts. Access to the books is obtained by appointment through the Director of the Museum School and the atmosphere is very informal – usually at art stool and an art desk in a hallway within earshot of all the goings on at the art school. But this source is invaluable. It mainly contains newspaper clippings from Boston area newspapers such as The Boston Globe, The Boston Herald, The Boston Transcript pertaining to alumni activities.

The scrapbooks were organized and maintained by employees at the Museum School and are indexed annually, further broken down in chronological order by month. Perhaps the most important clippings are those centered around the critical reviews offered by the art editors of the various newspapers. In these, we find a good source of descriptions of actual art works which help marry the actual works to their titles in the cases where there are no photographs. In addition, these scrapbooks are a valuable source of reproductions, as one, chosen from the particular exhibit, often accompanies the text and for the announcements of awards. Moreover, this is a significant source of information for:

○ the extant titles list;

- o the exhibition history;
- o the critical history
- o the awards history;
- o the correspondance lists; and
- o descriptions.

The Museum of Fine Arts, Boston

The Museum of Fine Arts, Boston, is located on Huntington Avenue next to the School of the Museum of Fine Arts and offers two areas pertinent to our exploration of American artists: its Library and the curatorial office of American Art.

The Library's card catalogue may be checked by artist's last name and by institution, any art institution at which the artist has exhibited since the Library maintains catalogues of exhibitions.

The curatorial office of American Art may be accessed by permission of the curator, by appointment. It maintains "vertical files" on artists represented in the museum's collection which may contain biographical information, reports and writings by graduate students, exhibition related materials, condition reports for the works in the museum collection and possible interview leads.

Galleries and Institutions

Galleries and institutions may be approached in person or by correspondance. If you visit the gallery in person, many directors will allow you to look through their vertical files for exhibition information and through their register books which offer details of exhibition history, art work dimensions and sale prices.

Every institution which you have encountered in your research should be contacted seeking both general information on the artist and his/her works, as well as verification of specific information already gleaned from prior research leads. An actual example of one such letter's text is shown in Figure 2.

Diane Kelleher
39 Westgate Road, #6
Chestnut Hill, MA 02167

Grand Central Art Gallery
Hotel Biltmore
Madison Avenue at 34th Street
New York, New York

Dear Sir,

As a graduate student at Boston University, I am engaged in researching the American artist, Lilian Westcott Hale (1881-1963).

I am writing to you because according to old Boston newspaper articles and records at the Archives of American Art, Boston, she either exhibited at your gallery or realized the sale of her works through your gallery on at least six occasions. In fact, your gallery appears to have been the most important and most frequent source of patrons for her art.

Enclosed is a list of the total extent of my information regarding Hale's relationship to the Grand Central Art Gallery. As you can see it is rather incomplete.

Would you be willing to look into your records, verify my information and send me any other information you have on Lilian Hale? I am particularly interested to know if she exhibited at your gallery at any other times; and, if so, the exact dates, titles, and with whom she exhibited; and who were her patrons.

Your help will be greatly appreciated. I look forward to hearing from you. Thank you so very much.

Sincerely

Diane Kelleher
Enclosure

Figure 2 – Sample Letter to Gallery

From:
Diane Kelleher
39 Westgate Road, #6
Chestnut Hill, MA 02167

Liliam Westcott Hale, 1881-1963
(Mrs. Philip Leslie Hale)

1916   December 27, 1916 – January of 1917 (exhibition title as yet not ascertained) – the work was "Portrait of Arthur Wilcomb"

1923   (exact date unknown) 30" x 22" oil entitled "Eleanor" sold to the Corcoran Gallery, Washington, D.C. (price is uncertain: according to Corcoran Gallery records it was $800.00; according to the Archives of American Art records -$1,000.00)

1924   May (exact date unknown) "Celia's Arbor" sold to the Metropolitan Museum of Art, New York for $500.00 (dimensions of painting unknown).

    May (exact date unknown) "Freezias Against the Snow" (patron not ascertained) for $650.00

    June (exact date unknown) "Ave Maria" sold to J.W. Donnelly of Birmingham, Alabama (price unknown).

    August (exact date unknown) "Spring Reverie" sold in conjunction with the "Founders' Show (patron not yet ascertained) for $1,000.00.

    August (exact date unknown) "Nancy on a Winter Afternoon" sold (patron not yet ascertained) for $1,800.00

1925   July 1 – 28 "Song of the Spheres" sold in conjunction with the Newport Art Association, Rhode Island (patron unknown) for $3,000.00

Figure 2 – Sample Letter to Gallery

1925   (Month, patron, and exhibit unknown for the following list of sales obtained at the Archives):

Easter Lilies – pencil	500.00
Black Eyed Susans	450.00
Song of the Spheres – drawing	350.00
"1830" – drawing	600.00
Study of a portrait	350.00
Nancy II	400.00
Study for a portrait	350.00
Book of Verses – drawing	600.00
Study of Ruth – drawing	450.00
R.M. – drawing	350.00
Valenciennes – drawing	350.00
Lady in a Regence Chair	500.00

1936   January 28 – February 8, "Exhibition of Drawings of Lilian Westcott Hale" at Grand Central Art Galleries – 15 Vanderbilt Ave., New York City. The titles of the works were:

Out on the Lawn
Buckthorn
The Black Tulip
Dedham Cottage
Terminus
The House Next Door
Dedham Steeple
Meeting House
Ancient English Elms
Venerable Branches
Dedham Steeple, Early Spring
Cherry Trees in Winter
Cineraria
The Dinosaurs

Figure 2 – Sample Letter to Gallery

(1936   January 28 - February 8, continued)
        Sun Over Ipswich Bay
        The Wood Shed
        Old Dedham House (Miss Margaret Williams was the
                lender)
        Pear, Elm, Pine
        The Wreath
        (Patrons, sale prices, media for the above remain to be
                ascertained.)

Figure 2 – Letter to Grand Central Art Galleries, New York, New York

Correspondence and Interviews

From your previous work with galleries and institutions, you will have compiled a list of possible contacts which will include those persons working in the gallery sector, but also patrons who purchased art from those galleries. Sometimes, galleries will divulge not only the names but the addresses of those patrons, to whom you may then write if you would like to request more information either in the form of a letter or an interview. This list of patrons will often include actual relatives of the artist which can be added to the list you derived from the artist's obituary.

Questionnaires are helpful at this stage of research. They can be mailed to patrons, relatives and friends of the artist too far away geographically to interview. Otherwise, they may be included in the actual interview with willing subjects. You may write to these patrons or phone them to request an interview.

Note: *It is helpful to communicate how many minutes you believe the interview will encompass at the beginning of the conversation so that patrons will not feel inordinately imposed upon.*

After a convenient date and time has been agreed upon for the interview, make sure that your questionnaire has both open and closed ended questions, and is suitable to being used in conjunction with the questions you have written on note cards to be asked during the interview. Also check your recording machine to be certain it is in working order.

Note: *You may ask during the phone call, or on the day of the interview, but be sure to ask if the patron, friend or relative has any objection to being recorded before you begin the interview. Experience teaches most people will have no objection to being recorded, and these recordings can be transcribed later into a notebook with very good and clear results. This is also your opportunity to ask to photograph patrons' works. A sample questionnaire for patrons is detailed below in Figure 3.*

<u>Lilian Westcott Hale – Questionnaire</u>

Name of Patron/Owner:

Address:

Patron's Education and Field of Interest:

Patron's Primary Occupation:

Hobbies:

Club Memberships:

Total Number of Works Owned:
    Paintings
    Drawings
    Other

Do you feel women or men prefer Lilian Hale's paintings?
___Men___Women___No distinction

Do you feel women or men prefer Lilian Hale's drawings?
___Men___Women___No distinction

Would you prefer to own one of Lilian Hale's paintings or drawings? Why?

Hypothetically, if you were forced to sell all of your paintings and drawings, would Lilian Hale's be among the first or the last you would sell?

    ___First   ___Last   ___Why?

What are the names of the other artists whose work you admire?

Have you purchased any works by the above artists?
___Yes ___No.

What is the title of the work/works you own?

Are you the original owner? If not, can you tell me the work's provenance?

How was the work acquired?
> Gift from the artist? If so, under what circumstances?

> Inheritance: If so, what influenced this gift's being given to you:
>> ___your expressed admiration for the work
>> ___it was a portrait of a member of the family
>> ___other.

> General Gift (wedding present, etc.)?

> Purchase:
> From: ___the artist; ___a gallery: ___an individual;
> ___auction; ___family.
> Name and address of the above:
> Date acquired:

Value over time:
> ___Purchase price (amount) _____year.
> ___Current insured value   _____year.
> Price you realized when you sold the work? _____

Figure 3 – Lilian Westcott Hale Patron Questionnaire

By utilizing this type of questionnaire you may ascertain trends among patrons of, for example, common club memberships. (Lilian Hale's patrons often belonged to the Dedham Garden Club and worked in the area of Finance). You may also ascertain provenance which is important for the Individual Works Survey which should be completed for every work uncovered in your research. This is helpful for the catalogue raisonne. The survey is shown in Figure 4.

<u>Individual Works Survey</u>

Title of Work:

Artist:

Present Owner/Location:

Collectioni:

Medium:

Dimensions:
___inches ___centimeters ___type of measurement (formal, sight)

Signed or not signed, and how:

Provenance:

Exhibition history:

Where reproduced:

Description:

Condition:

Back of work:

Figure 4 – Individual Works Survey

Note: *Biographical information and personal impressions of the artist may be garnered from specific questions during the interview process. Ask family members if they have written about the artist. (Lilian Hale's daughter, Nancy, wrote a helpful book called* The Life in the Studio *about her parents' lives as artists, and Hale's daughter-in-law completed a genealogical mapping of the family, helpful as Hale often painted her grandchildren.) Now, it's time to type up your chronology.*

WRITING

WHERE TO BEGIN

Where to begin the writing – whether with the appendices or the biographical sections or the art historical analysis – is a matter of personal choice. But one thing is certain, this is where all of your research information comes together.

Note: *Perhaps the simplest and one of the most interesting sections with which to start is the biography simply because you will be working a lot from the tape recorded interviews, which, if you have asked the correct questions, will contain interesting anecdotal incidents. This is also one of the more simple chapters since it is chronologically organized.*

A sample table of contents taken from *Enchantment: The Art and Life of Lilian Westcott Hale – Table of Contents* is reproduced in Figure 5. From the contents we glean that inclusions of several sections are mandatory to success of our book:

- the biographical section'
- sections broken down by distinct iconography;
- exhibitions;
- critical history;
- aesthetic principles;
- the art historical niche;
- the artist's particular contributions to technique and style;
- the latter part of the artist's life;
- the appendices, including the exhibition history and its notes;
- reproductions for the first page of each chapter.

Enchantment: The Art and Life of Lilian Westcott Hale
Table of Contents

List of Plates
Acknowledgement
Home, Heart and Heritage
Ties to New England
Style and Stylish Women
Snowy Landscapes
Bounty of Still-Life
Children and the Critics
Galleries and the Gold
Aesthetics of Beauty
The Linear Impressionist
Legacies: Ten and Eight
A Changing World
New Beginnings
Other Works
Appendices: Special Thanks to Special Friends
Chronology
Gallery and Museum Associations
List of Titles
History of Exhibitions
Notes to the History of Exhibition
Index to Reproductions
Bibliography

Figure 5: Enchantment: The Art and Life of Lilian Westcott Hale
Table of Contents.

Of course, every fact must be documented in the end-notes at
the end of each chapter.

Note: Sample appendices are given in the Appendices section.

PUBLISHING

STANDARD OR SUBSIDY PUBLISHING

Basically, you have two options when it comes to publishing: standard and subsidy publishing. If you chose standard publishing, you will need to construct a query letter by which means you will approach various publishers to ascertain the interest each might have in your manuscript. Query letters give the publishers sufficient information about you, your manuscript, and your qualifications to let them determine if they would like to further pursue your work. A sample query letter is shown in Figure 6. Lists of publishers and their addresses are available in the reference section of your local library. Your research librarian can help you find these. Figure 7 details those elements which should be included in your query letter.

Since many query letters end up receiving as responses a polite rejection letter, subsidy publishing may be your most advantageous option. For a predetermined fee, you may have your book printed by a publisher. In addition, depending upon which choices you make from their contract options, you may have them market your book to radio stations, television stations, the internet, and brick and mortar bookstores. Fees are also dependent upon how many reproductions you have in your book and the length of your book. Generally, fees will vary among subsidy publishers, for in addition, they have different programs, and it requires research to choose the best option for your manuscript.

Note: Sometimes upon copyrighting your book at the Library of Congress in Washington, D.C., subsidy publishers will obtain your "Form TX" and contact you offering their services.

The process of subsidy publishing is actually quite simple. After you chose your contractual options relative to marketing criteria and agree upon a price for your manuscript, you must submit the manuscript in hard copy or disk format.

Note: *Some subsidy publishers have requirements as to which software programs they will accept. Check with your publisher before writing your manuscript.*

Elements of a Query Letter

- Explain why you believe a particular editor would be interested in your work. (Perhaps this professional has edited works on similar topics or comes from the geographic location specific to your work.)

- State your title including the subtitle of your work.

- Describe the major focus of your work and its style.

- Describe the sources of your raw materials, for example, patron interviews, old newspaper articles).

- Explain how your book differs from the viewpoints of the competition.

- State the length of your manuscript.

- Offer a tentative delivery date.

- Detail your educational and professional qualifications for writing on this particular subject, and note any special connections (such as being the sole authorized biographer by the artist's estate).

- Convey enthusiasm for your project and thank the reader for his/her time.*

Figure 6 – Elements of a Query Letter

*See further Judith Applebaum's book, <u>How To Get Happily Published.</u>

After submission, the next step involves getting your book number and the "galley" – a proof of your book, which you will have to proofread for typographical errors. Each page should be read line by line, word for word. If the galley is acceptable, use the sign-off form, if not, use the "Galley Modifications Form" to make corrections to the text.

The cover often appears at the same time as the galley. Covers can be self-illustrated or initiated by the publisher. The choice is yours. But, this too will come with a form for sign-off, which is to be returned to the publisher. If both the galley and the cover are acceptable, your book will be printed and will arrive via private postal carrier when it is completed. At this time, you will be asked to select a price and royalty fee from pre-determined options. In addition, some publishers offer the author a specified number of free books. Otherwise, books may be obtained by request at brick and mortar stores, on the Internet, or by contacting the publisher. There is usually a reduced cost for ordering directly through the publisher.

For my books, I have been very happy with a firm called:

Author House
1663 Liberty Drive
Bloomington, Indiana 47403
1-800-839-8640.

CONCLUSION

Moreover, researching and writing a book for which there is no extant publication can be a very time-consuming and tedious process, yet it can also be exciting, especially during the interviewing phase, as well as one of the most rewarding endeavors you will ever undertake. There is no substitute for the pride you will feel as you look at your book on your own coffee table in your own home knowing that you created it all from scratch. And the royalty checks can be fun, too.

APPENDICES

Acknowledgements

Special thanks to Special Friends

...Neighbors, Friends and Relatives

Professor Cauthen
Mrs. Thomas Craven (Katu)
Mr. and Mrs. Mark Hardin
Professor William Nicols
Ms. Anne Shaughnessy
Mrs. Anson Howe Smith (Georgianna)
Mrs. Rutledge Vining
Mr. William Wertenbecker

...And From The Art World...

Addison Gallery of Art, Phillips Academy
N. Thurar and M. Cook

Albright Knox Gallery, Buffalo Academy of Fine Arts

Boston Athenaeum
Donald Kelley

Museum of Fine Arts, Boston
Laura Luckey

Brockton Art Center
Richard Minutello

Brookline Public Library
Judith Jackson

Diane Elizabeth Kelleher

Brief Chronology
Lilian Westcott Hale
1881-1963

December 7, 1880 or
December 6, 1881*

      Official birth certificate states Lillie Coleman Hale born to Harriet Clark and Edward Gardiner Westcott, Bridgeport, Connecticut. Other sources including, Hale herself (on her marriage certificate) identify her date of birth as December 6, 1881.

1880   Childhood. Spent in Connecticut. Sister dies. Father dies.

1895   Studying at Connecticut Academy of Fine Arts. Wins Paige Scholarship. Leaves high school to study at The School of the Museum of Fine Arts, Boston.

1896   Elected to membership of the Copley Society (originally, the Boston Art Students' Association of the School of the Boston Museum of Fine Arts).

1899   Engaged to Philip Leslie Hale, artist, faculty member at the Museum of Fine Arts School and descendent of historical family, including Edward Everett Hale (author of "The Man Without A Country").

1902   Edward Everett Hale marries Philip Hale and Lilian Westcott in Hartford, Connecticut. Couple honeymoons in Canada.

1905   Travel to France (1905/6).

1908   First one man show: "Drawings by Lilian Westcott Hale". Held in Boston at Rowland's Galleries, 402 West Boylston Street.

      First significant award: the Carol H. Beck medal. Received from the Pennsylvania Academy of the Fine Arts for "Miss Margaret Williams".

Gallery and Museum Associations

Ardeen Galleries, New York

Art Association of Newport (with Grand Central Art Galleries, New York)

Arlington Galleries

Art Club of Philadelphia, Pennsylvania

The Art Institute of Chicago, Illinois

The Boston Athenaeum, Massachusetts

Boston Art Club Galleries, Massachusetts

The Boston Museum of Fine Art, Massachusetts

The Boston Water Color Club, Massachusetts

The Buffalo Academy of Fine Art (Albright Knox Gallery), New York

The Carnegie Institute, Pennsylvania

The Concord Art Association, Massachusetts

Connecticut Academy of the Fine Arts (The Wadsworth Athenaeum)

The Copley Society, Massachusetts

The Corcoran Gallery, Washington D. C.

Dartmouth College, Robinson Hall, Hanover, New Hampshire

The Denver Art Museum, Colorado

Detroit Museum of Art, Michigan

Doll and Richards, Boston, Massachusetts

Duveen Galleries, New York

Grand Central Art Galleries, New York

First National Exhibition of American Art, Rockefeller Center, New York

The Guild of Boston Artists, Boston, Massachusetts

The Guild of Boston Artists Travelling Exhibitions (nationwide)

Hirschl and Adler Galleries, New York

Institute of Arts and Sciences, Manchester on the Merrimack, New Hampshire

M. Knoedler Galleries, New York

Lawrence Public Library, Massachusetts

MacIvory and Cassom, Boston, Massachusetts

Malden Public Library, Massachusetts

Mattatuck Historical Society, Waterbury, Connecticut

The Metropolitan Museum of Art, New York...

List of Titles

A

1860 (Sometimes called "1830")
A Baby (daughter, Nancy)
A Baby
Afternoon Tea
Agnes with Chain (Agnes Doggett Ruddy)
Agnes and Her Cat
Alice Behind the Looking Glass-
Alice Sit By The Fire
An Antique Ring
An Old Cherry Tree
Apple Blossoms and Narcissus
A Ray of Light
Ancient English Elms
Autumn Fruit and Flowers
Ave Maria

B

Barbara (Taylor)
Beatrice
Big Hat
Bill in Overalls (William Wertenbecker)
The Bird Screen
Bittersweet (Snowy Landscape)
Arthur Blake (holding cockleshell)
Harriet Blake (with pixie, in Moses)
Johnny Blake (seated, clasping knees)
Black-Eyed Susans
The Black Tulip
Bleeding Hearts

Diane Elizabeth Kelleher

A History of Exhibition
for Paintings and Drawings by
Lilian Westcott Hale

1902

Copley Society
Second Annual Exhibition of Contemporary Art
November 19 – December 19
Niagara, Morning
Niagara, Afternoon

1903

Pennsylvania Academy of the Fine Arts
72nd Annual Exhibition
January, 1903
Niagara, Morning
Niagara, Afternoon

1904   Inactive

1905   Inactive

1906

Pennsylvania Academy of the Fine Arts
101st Annual Exhibition
January 22 – March 16
As In A Looking Glass

Pennsylvania Academy of the Fine Arts
Water Color Exhibition
The Burnous
The Rose
The Shepherdess' Hat
Dora
The Little River Swan

Index to Reproductions

1860 (Alternatively, "1830)
>   Rose V. S. Berry, "Lilian Westcott Hale – Her Art", The American Magazine of Art, Vol. XVIII, No. 2, February 1927.

Agnes Ruddy with Chain
>   R. H. Ives Gammell, "An Appreciation of the Art of Lilian Westcott Hale", The Daily Progress, Charlottesville, Virginia, September 23, 1980.

Alice Sit By The Fire
>   The Literary Digest. Cover. N.Y. Funk and Wagnall's Co., Vol. 96, No. 2, Whole No. 1964, December 10, 1927.

Ave Maria
>   The Pennsylvania Academy of the Fine Arts, catalogue, "14th Annual Water Color Exhibition".

>   Grand Central Art Galleries, catalogue, "Exhibition of Paintings and Sculpture Contributed by The Founders of the Gallery", June 1924.

Barbara (Taylor)
>   Corcoran Gallery of Art, "Biennial Exhibition of Contemporary American Artists", December 1922.

The Bride
>   Corcoran Gallery of Art, catalogue. "Exhibition and Sale of Paintings for the Benefit of the Boston Museum of Fine Arts School" held at the Copley Plaza Hotel, April 1930.

The Brothers
>   Perkins, H. "Art Show at National Capital", Boston Evening Transcript, December 19, 1923.

Bibliography

Abbreviations: AE, -- Art Editorial
BMSS, -Boston Museum of Fine Arts, School Scrapbooks;
LR, -Letter of Response to DEK, Diane E. Kelleher;
R-, -Reproduction (of a work of Lilian Westcott Hale);
WHD-William Howe Downes

Academy. The Academic Tradition in American Art (N65-10F56), p. 245, R/Alice, 1927.

Addison Gallery of Art, Phillips Academy, N. Thurar, Asst. To Director, LR.

Albright Knox Gallery, Buffalo Academy of the Fine Arts, unsigned LR dated August 1978.

Alloway, Lawrence. *Topics in American Art Since 1945*, W.W. Norton and Co., Inc. (New York: 1975.

Arlington Galleries, New York. Catalogue, "Exhibit of Paintings and Drawings By Lilian Westcott Hale", March 1941.

American Heritage Magazine. "Boston Painters, Boston Ladies" by Carla Davidson, April 1972.

Archives of American Art, Boston. Microfilm including: Academy of Fine Arts Annual Report; Guild of Boston Artists; The Philip Leslie Hale Papers; Doll and Richards Gallery, Boston; Lilian Westcott Hale records.

Art Association of Newport. *Annual Reports.*

Boston Museum of Fine Arts, School of, Alumni Scrapbooks, especially *Vol. 5, 1911-13; Vol. 6 1914; Vol. 7, 1914-15; Vol. 8, 1915-16; Vol. 9 1916-18; Vol. 10 1918-19; Vol. 11, 1920-21; Vol. 13, 1924-26; Vol. 14, 1926-30; Vol. 16, 1932; Vol. 17, 1936, Vol. 18, 1940-50; Vol. 19, 1950-60.*

AE. "Mrs. Hale's Pictures", untitled paper, BMSS, March 9, 1920.

BIBLIOGRAPHY

Applebaum, Judith, *How to Get Happily Published*. New York, NY: HarperPerennial, 1992.

Kelleher, Diane Elizabeth. *Enchantment: The Art and Life of Lilian Westcott Hale*. Bloomington, Indiana: Author House, 2010.

www.ingramcontent.com/pod-product-compliance
Lightning Source LLC
Chambersburg PA
CBHW021938170526
45157CB00005B/2339